Spirit and Nature

By Richard A. Bowen

Published in the United States of America
by Ariadne Publishers, Brookfield, WI, U.S.A
© 1995, renewed 2019. All rights reserved.

ISBN: 9780964934313

DEDICATION

I dedicate this book to the Bliss-God that dwells in each one of us, to my Way-Shower Paramahansa Yogananda who taught me how to find happiness and balance, to my yoga teacher Yogacharya Oliver Black through whose example and love Yogananda's teachings became a living reality, and to my wife Karen whose love and positive attitude are a constant inspiration.

Spiritually Inspired Poems

A Vision of My Love

Before I went to sleep,
I had a vision of loving hearts
everywhere.
I felt my love flow out
to the hearts of all relatives,
to those that had passed on
and to those that yet remain:
mother, father, brother, sisters,
brothers-in-law, sisters-in-law,
mother-in-law, cousins,
nephews, nieces, aunts, uncles,
grandmothers, grandfathers,
great-grandmothers and great-grandfathers.

Then, in my mind's eye
I saw my dear friends,
male, female,
old, young,
living and dead;
and I loved them too.

I loved the sick, the homeless,
the drug-ridden, the hungry,
the murderer, the thief—
spread out
in a vast panorama of hearts,
some waiting to be loved,
some longing,
some too big to be loved,
some not sure of love,
some seemingly impossible to love,

1

yet I loved them.
My heart was warm with love,
and I knew I truly loved them,
that I had longed to love them.

And my love lay everywhere,
on every countenance,
on all bodies
and in all hearts;
It looked into all eyes.
My love gave to all, all of its love,
receiving all smiles and love in return.

At last, the vision
bathing in Its own thrill of love,
radiated love throughout the vastness of universes;
surrounding and inundating all entities
on all planets,
with Itself.

Although the female aspect of God is not commonly known in the West, it is a universal belief in the Orient.

Ode to Kali, the Mother of Creation

Om Kali! the Mother of Creation.
I bow to You now and forever more.
As I gaze lovingly
into Your shimmering face,
I see the workings of creation,
the perils of destruction,
and the tranquility of preservation
at once.
Your body shines with movement:
a million laser rays blaze forth.

Won't You stop Your triune duties
to bestow a thimble-full of
Your infinite love upon me?

This devotee seeks
nothing but Your love.
Like the bee who, in the midst
of the forest,
seeks out the farthest fragrant flower,
I seek Thee.
O sweet Mother! Your love beams
like gravity,
and irresistibly pulls all things
and all beings
magnetically toward You.
When I look at You,
Your straight and perfect teeth

seem to be made of
concentrated stardust,
and glow like
self-illuminated diamonds;
Your eyes, whose irises contain
all colors, all shades, all hues,
plead for help unblinkingly;
and Your hair entangles in it
the physical, astral,
and causal universes;
and Your feet tread the paths toward
ever-blossoming creation, preservation
and the furies of destruction.

Constantly busy with Thy "housework,"
Your hands are forming endless tracts
of matter and space,
the yet unmanifested existences in the
vast majestic ocean
of eternal consciousness;
You are faithfully
perpetuating calmness and joy
in all Thine abundance enjoyed
by life-forms throughout the universe;
and with a movement of Your hand,
You destroy worn-out, useless worlds
whose sparks of life have gone out
and which You sweep
under the rug of agelessness
to be resurrected, perhaps, someday,
in new versions of Your cosmic play.

O Divine Mother!
Stop Thy perpetual work!
Allow me to bask for a single moment
in the outpourings of Thy heart
and I will be free.

Light on Life

O Infinite Spirit!
Thou art Light,
Thou art Life.
Thou and I are one.

Thou art Happiness;
I am happy.
Thou art Peace;
I am peaceful.
Thou art Abundance;
I am prosperous.
Thou art Bliss;
I am blissful.
Thou art Love;
I am loving,
I am loved.
Thou art Immortality;
I am an immortal.

O Infinite Beloved!
Thou art ever calling me
back to my Home
And I hear Thy voice,
O my Soul,
O my Bliss,
O my Blessedness,
O my Own.

During meditation, the heart and lungs slow. The resulting freed-up energy is then used for higher, more cerebral purposes.

Mother Nature and the World of Men

I walked along the muddy bank—
the air sweet and still. My eye drank
green and the rush's dew. I saw
the water flow, ebb, and draw,
winding along the broadening bend
to meet the stony rapid's wend.

But no birds or fowl or fish were there
to fill the water, woods, or air.
So becoming utterly still,
I sat on the bank until
I noticed in a flowering tree
a hummingbird above;
a chipmunk appeared atop a rock
before bounding over to a shock
of cattails. And a pair of ducks
swam by. But suddenly breath sucks
itself in and my heart moves again—
back to the ambitious world of men.

I Have Become Thee

Living beyond
needs,
thoughts,
and feelings,
I have become
success,
abundance,
happiness,
joy,
love,
bliss,
blessédness,
and peace.

I find no use for skepticism,
no time for discussion,
no room for speculation;
there is nothing to add or subtract.
For my time is now!
my life is now!

And I long to share my life with all.
No longer needing to be loved,
I want to love.
No longer needing succor or relief,
I want to comfort and console.
No longer wanting to receive,
I want to facilitate and give.
No longer wanting to teach,
I want to learn.

O Infinite Spirit!
Bless me that I may follow in Thy ways
of freedom,
ever-newness, understanding, knowledge, wisdom,
and fathomless peace.

Take me on a new life-journey
filled with divinely-inspired adventure:
never-before viewed vistas and horizons,
newly acquired soul-friends,
and truly helpful endeavors.
May the time I have in this existence
prove to be charged with
vitality, energy, zeal,
prosperity, health, and creativity.

With Thy blessing,
I will positively succeed in the world
with all worthwhile endeavors
and noble pursuits.
And I will surely renew my thoughts
to reflect only the good,
only Thy divine thoughts.

May my actions promote
Thy wise actions;
my words, Thy sweet words,
my love, Thy all-consuming Love,
my joy, the Divine ever-new joy
that knows no end
and has had no beginning
and will forever be in this world
and in the World beyond all worlds.

May I realize in all feeling,
thoughts, words, and deeds,
in all space, in all matter,
and in all bliss, that it is Thou O my living God
that I love; and it is Thou
in whom I pray,
and Thou in whom I live.

I surrender to Thee; I am one with Thee,
now, forever, and forever more.
Om. Peace. Bliss. Amen.

Moonlight Walk

I took a walk in the moonlight.
Stark, bright the light lit up
the dark. The snow lay on the ground,
solid, frozen, hard-to-the-foot;
white beams reflecting, stars
shining, moon smiling down.
Beams shooting, bouncing, streaming
at eyes used to blackness; waking,
illuminating, opening
with pure energy-forces ur-
gently moving inside my mind.
Scintillating, evanescent,
shifting, sweeping back and forth
to wake the cells of eye and brain,
body and skin cells that strive for light,
and thoughts appearing to manufacture their own,
and cells of blood, muscle, and bone.
Basking them in new rays reflected
from remote sun in far-off space,
which seems empty and devoid
of light, like the night until the moon
rains in to charge and churn it up.
The blackness of night delivers us
like restless thoughts deceive us
into believing
that behind our shuttered eyes
there is nothing.
Yet now, mind is still.
Starlight peeps in, playful,
soothing, joyful, mellow, indicating
astral realms beckoning with full

11

energy fields flickering slowly;
proof of huge astral world
forming, governing, reflecting, and joining
the physical, and causal world above.
Love brings and holds them together,
my love, and, like this three-world play,
we shall not part.

Endless Life

Endlessly quaffing wavelets of Bliss
on shores of Divine Mother's love,
I'm unaware of a serious side of this play
which She's producing to entertain
Her cherished children,
who are too busy
to return Her Divine love to Her
and get into trouble, crying and fighting
and wailing while nursing their desire-born hurts,
and inflicting pain on their lives, their loves,
their neighbors and families,
their co-workers and friends
who doing it too,
reinforce one another
with their actions and thoughts,
and mindless of them,
allow this to pass to the children,
unheeded, as the habit goes on,
until someone wakes up and says
to everything
"Stop!"
and it ceases to roll,
and all becomes calm, soothing, serene,
tranquil, mellow, buoyant and loving,
and happiness and warmth arise
from clear thinking, and common sense wins out over
craziness,
and I'm looking on, embroiled too,
while feeling compassion and love
for myself
and for them.

Everything Comes From Thee

O Father, everything comes from Thee.
Man makes nothing,
not a grain of wheat
nor a blade of grass.
He only rearranges Nature
to suit his purpose.

Thus I seek Thee,
the Giver of all gifts,
the Creator of all things.

As a divine son,
I demand sustenance from
Thy glorious sunlight,
the fragrant oxygen,
bountiful, wholesome foods,
and the thirst-quenching waters.

In them may I realize
Light, Vitality, Vigor, and Life.

Give me mental efficiency,
calmness, creativeness,
love, warmth,
thought-power, will power,
and divine understanding.

As I receive these precious gifts,
teach me to share them
with my brothers and sisters
so that they too feel Thy bounty
and share in Thy abundance.

For what good would be Thy abundance
if Thou didst not share it with Thy children,
the plants, insects, animals, and man?
Truly it would be useless and wasted.

Now, I humbly thank Thee
for remembering me
so that I can share
in the wealth of universes.

I know that everything is mine,
that all space is my home;
that all love is in my heart,
and all creativity and inspiration
is in my soul.

I am truly Thy divine Son, Daughter,
Brother, Sister;

and Thou art truly my own
Mother, Father,
Friend and Beloved.

Let me not forget this.

God Must Sustain Me

O Father and Mother of Universes,
I am Your little child.
You must take care of me;
I give myself unconditionally
to Your care.

Like a little earthly child,
who does not take care of himself
but depends solely on his
earthly father and mother,
I, as a divine child, am depending entirely on You,
my Heavenly Father and Mother.

Now grave doubt begins to assail me;
fear darkly comes upon me.
I cry out for Thy succor:
"Thou who hast everything, all stars, universes, solar
systems, planets, all bounty and earthly wealth—
I supplicate thee!

"Thou dost knowest all mankind's needs;
Thou dost knowest my family's needs
and all my own needs
even better than I know them myself.

"I who own nothing,
who hast come into this world
with nothing
and who will leave it with nothing,
beseech Thee for sustenance.

"Supply me with all my needs
according to Thy will.
I offer Thee infinite faith;
I sacrifice the trembling worries
and the timid doubts
that attempt to invade my mind.
Take them.
I will do anything that Thou biddest me to do.

"But even though I do nothing,
I am a recipient
of all the riches
of the heavens
for I am Thy child.

"Bless me;
remove these doubts and fears
from my brain.
Likewise remove all laziness and sloth
from my life,
for I want to be like Thee,
ever busy in the office of creation,
forming new worlds,
new experiences,
new beings.

"I want to assist Thee in Thy work,
someday being a co-creator with Thee,
invigorating, energizing, inspiring
new life-forms
to entertain and to be entertained
so that all can have great fun!
once Your strong delusion has been over-come."

You see Father,
I have naught but
Thy best intents in my mind.
Now I surrender to Thee
and Thy plans
for me, for my family, my world.

Won't You whisper
Your sweet encouragement,
blessings and love to me?

The Yogi's Favorite Time of Day

Now the endless living light
begins to fade away
the dusk is falling over head
to end an autumn day.
All is silence ever-new,
the joy, the love, the peace,
sun setting through the trees,
the blueness of air in space.
Of godliness, of breath, of inner search,
the east wind speaks and sails.
Cutting sound and whipping 'round,
then tranquil; calm prevails.
Blue dusk light surrounding me,
the blue of my Krishna of yore.
The yogi's favorite time of day,
to meditate on heavenly shore.
Absorbing brimming inner peace,
I muse in ecstasy—
divine bliss flowing everywhere—
shooting through holy body.
And deep sacred Om all 'round,
universal intelligence,
reverberating sound abounds,
giving living soul solace
to eager devotee bee
who loves to be with Thee,
who loves to be with Thee.

The Inner Castle

I have built an inner castle.

Constructed of blocks of
positive noble thoughts,
the granite-like walls of the castle
guard a treasure trove of
Divine Love, Peace,
Understanding, Goodwill,
Success, Prosperity and Abundance.

Surrounded by a mote filled with
the still waters of faithfulness,
I reside in this castle protected from
the enemies of negative thoughts, bad habits, ignoble
desires, failure, lack, boastfulness,
low self-esteem, fear, distain, jealousy, envy,
greed, prejudice and hate.

Even though my soldiers
of good are seemingly fewer,
I triumph and defeat any siege
mounted against me;
for I know that my well-trained army
of noble thoughts and deeds,
including those from past lives,
is specially skilled
in the art of spiritual warfare
to defeat the hordes
of marauding negative forces
sent by *Maya*.
Shooting ignorance and fear on sight,

my army is equipped with
the state-of-the-art, all-powerful weapons of
will and cosmic energy
to vanquish vice forever.
When these forces are called to battle,
they respond with indomitable fury and power;
it is as though the energy of a million suns
is concentrated at my fingertips
for the sole purpose of conquering
the pitiful alien group gathered
to attempt an attack on me.
Not knowing the sudden,
hidden strength of my battalions,
at the mere sight of my soldiers of volition,
the foe is scattered, tattered and ravaged
beyond the ability of anyone or anything
to regroup it.

Having successfully turned back all sieges,
I march forth from my noble inner home castle
with a banner of goodness,
recruiting all others like myself
who desire to be free
from the tyranny of negativity.
I gather a vast multitude of divine recruits,
who have in their minds a single objective:
to annihilate all that is negative,
first from the shores of their own minds,
then from Earth,
and finally from the universe
where evil has clandestinely entrenched itself
heedless of the Voice
which from the Beginning proclaimed,
"Ye are Gods!"

As the leader of my forces of Good,
I will not shrink from my responsibility
to my brethren,
for it has been shown to me that
although men and death may attempt
to separate us,
my brother soldiers and I are one,
even as my Father and I are One.
Just as a mother loves her child
even if he is a murderer,
so I love even those who have in the past
harbored negative thoughts
toward me and my fellow men.

Returning to my castle after being victorious
in the Battle of the Ages,
I intend to completely enjoy my life
of peace, prosperity, divine love,
understanding, humility, wonderment,
ecstasy, helpfulness and fun.
For the inner enemies have been destroyed,
and all outer threats have laid down
on the field of forgetfulness,
never to rise up again.

My Everlasting Love

I have built a monument of love for Thee
on granite blocks of devotion.
I have stilled my restless thoughts of Thee
on the wavelets of emotion.

Where once my thoughts were devoid of Thee
I have set into gentle motion
my ever-whispering love for Thee
inside ev'ry fragrant notion.

I search on and on for Thee
in fathomless faith-filled ocean.
The Pearl of Great Price are Thee
residing in soul's promotion

of higher and higher perceptions of Thee
beyond worldly commotion.
Evermore I long to make love to Thee
in my temple of remotion.

I Am Free

I am free of my past,
of my family name,
of past actions,
of old beliefs,
of past thoughts and habits of thought,
of karma good and bad.

I am free of past lives,
of who I was,
what I had,
what I lost,
whom I hurt,
whom I helped,
of victories and defeats.
I am free of future concerns,
of what I shall do for a living,
of who I shall meet,
what I shall wear and eat,
and where I shall live.

I am free to live in the present.

Free of all bias and prejudice,
my brothers are
black, brown, red, white, and yellow;
they are
Hindu, Moslem, Jew,
Christian, Buddhist;
worker, soldier,
clerk, manager, president.
I feel my heart

loving them all
as I love myself

All Nature is mine:
plants, trees, minerals;
water, sky, air;
moon, planets, and stars.

All beings are my relatives:
birds, the horse, the mouse;
the tiger, elephant, and sheep;
bear, woodchuck, and monkey:
fish, goat, fly and gnat.
I am loving them all
as the manifestations
of a Living God.

I am free of all physical and mental disease.
Bursting with initiate, strength,
virtue, fortitude, inspiration, and zeal,
I express warmth, kindness,
frankness, diplomacy,
truthfulness, and divine love.

I am free of attitudes:
boredom, listlessness, restlessness;
sarcasm, envy, contempt;
lust;
attraction to pleasure,
aversion to pain.

Yet I am free to feel the pain of others,
the homeless,
the drug-ridden,
the hungry,
the sick,
the abused.

I am free to feel the joys of others,
the newly-weds,
father, mother,
grand-parent,
athlete
and scholar.

Free of preferences,
likes and dislikes;
at liberty to enjoy all that my Father gives me,
free of all thoughts of lack and poverty,
I am aware of abundance everywhere
and I accept my unceasing gifts now,
with gratitude.

Serving, helping—
I share that which I receive
with others.

Free of meditation, prayer,
thought, emotions,
bodily sensations;
free only to Be,
I am boundless, limitless,
omnipresent, omnipotent.
Love,

Happiness,
Peace
and Bliss
I am.

I am
free!

The soul, although ever free, gets caught up in desires during reincarnational earthly sojourns and becomes attached to the body and senses. By yoga, the devoted practitioner retraces his footsteps to the heavenly abode from whence he came. Traveling mentally back up the spine (the "silvery stream"), the spiritual eye (or third eye, star of Bethlehem or star of the East) becomes inwardly visible, at the point between the eyebrows, as a white star in a field of blue inside a golden halo or circle. He again feels the ecstasy which is his natural Self When he reaches this heavenly abode, the yogi "repents," never again wanting to get caught in a net of desires. Again and again, comparing this heavenly bliss to earthly pleasures, finally he forsakes the body and sense attachment. Thus in a state of constant joy, he remains in "heaven" perpetually.

Soul Wanderings

Celestial Light of stardust deep,
I woefully allowed my soul to sleep
And to wander amidst dreary lairs
And to play with scorching sensory fires.
Awakened now from fitful dream
I follow the single silvery stream;
To bathe in restful, care-free peace,
That whispers of sweet soul release
And longed-for powerful burning bliss
Beyond the suffering of soul's distress
Into the blue, golden-ringed sky
Teaching subtle consciousness to fly
Through blazing white-starred center space
Where earthly sorrow doth my soul erase.
Winging me far from sorrowful sphere,

Where gladness doth fill th' narrow ear
And booming Om calling to heavenly home
Never more myself to roam.

Part II

Bolts of ecstasy shooting through veil-like screen
Pseudo-happiness ne'er shown again
Letting my soul ring truly free
Desire shot down; flying up to Thee.
Weathering trials of torment's night
To reach the field of soul's delight,
Feeling the bliss that is made of You
in ecstasy piercing golden ring, field of blue
Through white star into shimmering astral land
With lights flashing from celestial hand.
May I leave Thee never again
We travel in time down earthly sands,
follow incarnation's frightful course
To be born repeatedly to soul's remorse.
Instead by free will I choose Eternal Bliss
Forever abandoning desire's deep abyss.

Divine Mother's Return
(written after being blessed with feeling the Divine Mother's love in meditation)

O Mother,
do not deny me the precious gift of Your presence.
Come to me again;
allow my aching astral senses to adore Thee.
Reveal Thyself again and again
until I can see, hear, taste, touch and smell
naught but Thee.

Your presence I require.
All is plentiful, all is abundance
when I feel Your slightest touch,
when I quaff the ever-new subtlety
of Your fragrant Being.

Reveal Thyself onto me everywhere,
O Divine Mother,
so that I may share Thee with my brothers,
for they too unknowingly long for Thy touch;
Thy mesmerizing joy;
Thy unceasing, delightful joy.

Play hide and seek with me no more.
My life cannot be meaningful
unless Thou dost fill it with meaning,
every moment, every hour, every day.

Mother, when Thou didst visit me,
Thy loving touch,
and transfiguring embrace

changed forever my thoughts,
feelings, attitudes and desires
so that now they are filled always
with naught but longing for Thee.

Thy hands, Thy face, and Thine eyes
bespeak the joy for which I live.
Engulf me now—guide me—
For Thou art my goal, my life, my love
forevermore.

Tarry not in Thy return to me,
for I wait silently, on the fields
of meditation and activity,
always desiring Thee alone.

Beloved, Thy thoughts surround my soul;
my thoughts reflect Thy love;
Thy heart murmurs love songs
as my heart recalls Thy love evermore.

In the recesses of my brain
and in my ever-loving heart throbs,
I will hold and forever cherish
Thy gift of eternal Love.

Help me to think of Thee
even though there are times
I think of Thee not.

Expand my love for Thee
to encompass all things
and all beings.

31

Help me to see Thy hand
working behind all the scenes
of this motion-picture show of life.

In eternity, in ever-new joy
I shall find Thee,
whenever I ardently look
for Thee.

Mother, I know that
Thou art calling me home
with nothing but Thy sacred love;
and I long to hear Thy voice,
as I long to see Thy face reflecting
heavenly Omnipresence.

Your sacred Grandeur
shall I behold
only if Thou wilt bless me.

With Thy Grace, Justice and Mercy
ever persuade me back Home
where I know
Thou art waiting for me.

My Guru, Paramahansa Yogananda

O my Guru, thou didst bring to the West
From the hoary past of India
The modern scientific techniques of
soul-realization.

But more than that, thou brought thyself
The embodiment of Divine Love.

The essence of Divine Love are thee,
Holding together the atoms of bliss,
That contains within it all the attributes
Of God the Father, the Son
and the Holy Aum Vibration.

Thou art the Lover,
The act of Loving,
And the Belovéd.
Thou art mine.

Bless me that I live in constant remembrance
Of thy admonition of worldly life,
Of obliviousness to thy bliss pipings,
Of spiritual laziness and apathy.

Instead, charge me, as thy unique contribution
To the science of Yoga,
The Energization Exercises, doth charge the body,
With daily renewing efforts to know thee,
And through thee the Blesséd Lord.

As the "speaking voice of silent God,"
Thou has led me from
The shores of discontentment and futility to
The realm of bliss and light.

Ever lead me, my brothers, sisters,
And all sentient beings
To the abode of Bliss,
Never becoming unconscious or oblivious
Of the One who sent thee.

O thee, my blessed Guru,
Who without looking back left all—
Family, friends, home—
To start a new spiritual family and a new
Life never before lived in the West,
Thy example has in itself
Led many others along the path
Of Self-Realization and will do so evermore
As long as the life of man
Strives to better itself.

O Guru sublime,
Thou art ever the shining star in my life.
One day we shall merge together
In the cosmic sea, going "no more out,"
Ever bathed in bliss, in celestial light,
In all solacing Divine Love.

Bless me that thou wilt always be
In my spiritual sight,
Always an ever-living presence;
And thy teachings a living Truth,
Thy love an ever-joyous feeling in my heart.

Om, Peace, Bliss, Amen.

Clear Light
(written after attending a yoga retreat)

Pigeon river winding through woods,
rushing through the falls.
Morning misty Lotus Lake,
tea and showers, all!

Rejuvenation rites—
vortexes a-whirl.
Ever-youthful living fountain,
sacred *pranas* swirl.

Breaking fast with spiritual fruit,
murmured conversations.
Fellowship and quiet laughter,
before blissful meditation.

Incense wafting, votives glow,
late-morning ecstasy.
Reedy organ, tablas, bells;
voices chanting, harmony.

Wisdom words flow from the lips,
of Baba, William, Dennis.
Yogis practice *pranayama*,
diving deep in inner silence.

******

Light beams spread o'er the hills,
as mists give way to sun.
Sharing, conversation, laughter—
the yogis eating lunch!

Walking in th' freshened air,
clearing mind and brain.
"Awake and ready!" our battle cry,
on spiritual terrain.

Entering high vibrations
of sunlit healing Lodge.
Past mistakes laid on altar-shrine,
doubts, fears, lives to dislodge.

Devotion pouring out to Lord,
Father, Mother, Beloved;
Ascended Masters, I AM Presence,
Jesus, Mary, Gurus blesséd.

Evoking, chanting many names
for the All-Blesséd One.
Casting out devotion prayers,
becoming saintly God-sons.

Each makes intention known,
as scientific breathwork starts.
Spiritual force breaks blockages
op'ning vast, panoramic hearts.

Sharing inner spiritual adventure;
feeling soul release,
essence of flowers' soothing touch
brings unfathomed peace.

******

Meditation in tears of joy,
as earthly night-time falls.
Candles lit on altar-hearts;
Baba's wisdom fills us all.

Last day's Sunday service,
circle chanting, sharing.
Crying tears of gratitude
for the Masters' visible caring.

Heartfelt hugs exchanged,
never parted in Spirit—Om.
Love overflowing, evermore.
Ascension, our Heavenly Home.

A *Christmas Poem for Karen*

The snows of Christmas quietly fall
From wispy sky above.

Me beside you, feeling your love,
I answer your sweet sacred call.

Home to Him our Spirit we go;
Blesséd Joy marks the way.

Hand in hand together today,
Yet in rare secret heart we sow

Dear loving thoughts each harbors within;
Blesséd feeling that knocks on the door.

May we blaze our paths together, then,
Living in His Love evermore.

The Dream of Life
(for Karen on St. Valentine's Day)

As I go through this dream of life
with you, my love,
it is wondrous to behold the fabric of it
from another perspective—
your eyes.

We meditate and work,
sleep and dream—
always knowing that
we rest in the Divine Mother's arms.

Yet it is a game of Hers
to sometimes make us think
we are apart from Her;
She is indeed a jealous Lover,
playing Her mysterious game
of hide and seek.

Perhaps this is Her way to keep us
ever aware of Her seemingly capricious love.
But in our hearts, may we know
without doubt,
that Love *is* the Divine.

And sharing this Love
makes the dream a delight,
however unreal.
And that sharing this Love
unfailingly leads to the Bliss
of our commingled souls.

To Eternal Karen, My Love

The ethereal bliss-pipings of thy heart
hath called me.
They have gently coaxed me
to come and live with thee
and to share the Divine Love that flows ceaselessly
from the heart-cask of our one Divine Father.

What serenity! What mellow joy resides here!
An eternity of love, of peace, of fun and hope
hath sprung forth!

Never-ending vistas of bright, sun-lit joy
spread out from our hearts,
which have become one.

The evanescent aurora dissipates and dissolves into
mutually shared clouds of Light
that sing an ever-new song of Love.

Poem on St. Valentine's Day

Love.
Gentler than the water
in the flowing stream,
as warm as a soft summer breeze.

You and I, feeling love divine,
living in harmony
with cosmic scheme—
how sweet!

Yet how profound,
this joyous love life of ours
when shared between ourselves
and with a love-hungry world.
And how it makes our hearts ache
and our love increase
to see another being suffer.

We are traveling a road
of love, naught else,
which leads to heavenly realm;
let us not tarry
for the Stealer of hearts
is calling us
to rejoin Him there.

I love you
with His love
that never ends
nor diminishes;
a divine love,

which grows
evermore loving, joyous,
sweet and fulfilling
until we, the lovers,
are aglow with love.

I love you
as the joyous being that you are;
I love you
for your strength and beauty,
courage and intelligence,
your graciousness and charm—
God-qualities all.
I love you for spontaneity and fun,
for appreciativeness and humility,
for striving and patience,
and for the Divine Mother's love
personified in you.

No time to reflect now,
no time to dwell
as we flow forward
in a stream of love,
in a gentle breeze of love,
in the heart's feeling of love,
I pray.
I love.
You.

Prayer to Mahavatar Babaji

O deathless Babaji, who has remained
in physical form as an example
to all spiritual aspirants, I bow to you.
Grateful am I that thou hast been working,
alongside Jesus Christ,
for the fulfillment of the divine plan
for the present age.
O great master who plays with time and space
like a child plays with bubbles,
may I always take heart from thy example,
and solace from thy divine work.
I bow to thee again and again
O blesséd Mahavatar.

Prayer to Lahiri Mahasya

Bless me that I receive thee, O Lahiri Mahasya,
in the Light of Kriya Yoga.
Bless my practice
of this liberating technique that it may free me
from the strong delusion in life.
Let nothing, seemingly good nor bad,
stand in the way of my sacred practice
and my ever-expanding spiritual perceptions.

Bless my yoga meditation
that I fully realize the Divine, *this moment.*
Following your example,
may I become fully illuminated
yet still diligently perform
my duties in the world.
And by my example may I help lead others
to the divine science of yoga
which thou personifies.

Om. Peace. Bliss. Amen.

Nature Inspired Poems

Antiques

Antiques fill the room,
Things of fine age.
Soon they'll fill a page
Of my life.

Chairs once sat upon,
Polished brown wood.
Think back
If I only could
A time that swiftly passed.

Look through dusty windows;
A world changed so very much.

Now I look around,
The pieces turn to dust.
Leave now, I must
Return to my time.

I can live today.
I can live today.
I will live today.

The Subtle Scare

Once, I know, she read
Something about a ghost
And a house.

Having picked it up
On her own accord,
It seemed to influence her more

And she became afraid.
Of course, she'd been
Reading at night, alone

And that, I've known long
Can produce such fright
Especially in one with a fragile heart;

That is, one who keeps
His feelings keen to what is
Hidden and what is seen.

The Chickadee on the Plank Porch

The chickadee dances on
the wooden plank porch.
Sails up to birch.
Pecks at a seed.
Hops to pine next-door.
Taps on a pine cone.
Empty.
Flits onto the rail,
wings flutter madly.
Small swoop to ground.
Scratches at a dead leaf;
cocks head to left.
Lofts up to cedar branch;
inspects smooth leathery leaf.
Satisfied.
Glides back to porch.
Finds birdseed.
Wary.
Cracks it.
Downs it instantly.
Struts one step across the planks.
Pecks at more seed.
Trusting, cracks another.
Downs it quickly.
Cracks, eats, cracks, eats.
Done.
Launches back up to the cedar.
One look at window. Gone.

The chickadee,
bursting with energy, joy, fun!

49

Charged with excitement,
happy, smart, dapper,
going about his natural work.

O man! May we too live
bursting with energy,
excitement, and bliss;
feeling joy, power and happiness.

The Kettle Moraine

We drove out to the Kettle Moraine, you,
the wind and I. The city with its pace,
its noise, faded and dissolved into blue,
silence, stillness, beech, birch, Queen Ann's lace,
oak, sumac, tamarack, and the waning grace
of autumn. We saw a black-capped chickadee
dance from ironwood to pine to apple tree

and then startled a dozen spotted thrush out
onto the gray horizon. The afternoon
painted the sky pink, the pearl-colored dusk
descended. Everything grew still and cool
while we walked by the crystal marshy pool
where the acrid water stood brown and clear.
I took a stick and struck the bottom near

the bank. Stoic and massive, the limestone made
the staff sound solid in my hand. The path—
winding through the woods atop a moraine,
the round smooth stones rolling loose beneath
our tread—led us along the country
hills where we sailed our thoughts of joy and light
past the valley of the foolish dreams of night.

The Snow One Night

White flakes slam softly onto my thigh,
Crushed underfoot and packed as I stride.
I wade through the wetness as the heavy, sticking stuff
Rains down hard and hits my cheek.

Houses silently stand-up against the storm.

The windy weather wakes the neighbors,
Dreaming in their white warm beds.
Shifting like bears in air, the breath of sleep;
Branches clicking on their crystal windows.

Street lights reflecting white snow shine.

In the lighted night, boys throw snowballs,
And make snow castles and snowmen,
Till someone from inside the house scolds them, shouting,
"It's late! You boys come inside!"

Sharp sounds fall muffled into the snow.

A car creaking under a cake of white,
Rocked and pushed and roundly cursed.
Three men in boots but no-gloves; frosty clouds
Of breath billowing from their mouths.

Snow diminishes the city's movement, sound, and lights.

Slow-moving, struggling, bundled-up people
Venturing out to shop and to work

Even on a snow-filled night when the weather excuses
Nearly everything else in the world.

Tragedy and happiness, no second to the storm.

Babies born; old ones die.
Sirens. Red lights blinking, flashing,
Slicing through tons of wind and storm-
filled air, warning of dangers.

The night grows deeper, the storm quiets down.

Late night, the storm overcomes
The din and activity of the main-made world.
Its own remains: suddenly clear air –
The conquering blizzard has nearly spent itself.

The sunrise will make the scene seem like summer.

Hit with golden gleaming sunlight,
Morning attempts to hide and gloss over
The darkness and fear we felt in the storm last night.
I rise up in bed and look out.

The pristine wondrous world lies lustrous before me.

Tinley Park Illinois

We sauntered along
dust-filled paths
that wound through glens of auburn.
Feathered dry leaves from honey locust trees
tried in vain to block the fall sunlight.

We rode over the
crystal bridge
through the concrete night of stars.
The city lay clean and white below;
a diamond sea of cars rushed away.

Then you sang to me
little songs
that remind me now and shall ever
remind me that you are always near—
that you *are* the paths, the leaves, the bridge.

Door County Snowdrifts

On a February Sunday,
it is my desire to go outdoors for some air
before it gets too dark.
The thermometer reads five degrees.

At exactly 3:00 p.m.,
I put on boots, coat,
hat, scarf, and mittens.
As I leave the house, I notice the camera
reposing on the table
near the door.

Stepping onto the wooden porch,
I unintentionally disturb
the late-afternoon quiet.
No wind.
Walking briskly, I stride
onto the winding,
snow-covered driveway
and the road.

Shortly, a van-full of bundled-up people
pass me,
driving fast,
heading to Cave Point Park
where Lake Michigan waves,
pounding against limestone,
have created grottos—
now ice-enshrined.
In the distance,
the faint hum of a snowmobile.

Resting 30 degrees above the horizon,
the sun is beginning to set.
My boots softly compact the powdery snow.
On my right,
abandoned-for-the-winter homes; the left,
silent woods calf-high in snow.

At the boat launch,
in order to gaze out
on the lake's arctic-like ice pack,
I attempt to make my way to the pier
but the snow has drifted knee-high
in the parking lot.
I look for a path to transverse it.
There—near the far edge;
an incessant Lake Michigan wind
has blown away most of the snow;
sight-seers have improved the path the more.

I trace their steps,
the wind picking up.
Reaching the shore,
I look out onto the frozen bay from the pier.
Long cirrus clouds
spread over solid blue;
ice white;
dark-green-and-red cedar trees
pack the shorelines.

My mind escapes
into the solitary landscape
and then comes to rest.
I breathe in the cold lake air.

Turning to leave,
I behold a snow drift,
built up from the snow
that blew off the lake last night,
its edges sculpted and shaped by a stiff wind.
Cool afternoon sunlight
shines on its curves;
waves and clefts are alternately lit and shadowed
by the weak rays,
the powdery snow too cold
to be melted by them.

Absorbing the natural snow sculpture,
in awe of its contoured form
and the freedom used in its creation,
I want to capture its beauty somehow.
But the camera
resides at home,
on the table near the door.
I linger by the drift.

Retracing my steps,
I begin my walk back to the road.
Turning toward Clark Lake,
I see a second powdery drift,
the sun sculpting its contoured form, too.

I turn around and fast-walk
the third-of-a-mile back to the house.
Inside, I drop the camera
into my coat pocket.

Closing the door behind me,
I trek past the lakeshore homes
and the silent woods.

Shadows are criss-crossing
the boat ramp parking lot on my return.
I plunge onto the foot path
but stride evermore slowly in silence.

The curves of the snowdrift near the shore
have vanished into blue shadows.
The contoured edges, the clefts,
and the curves are indistinct.

I dash out of the ramp area and back to the road.
The roadside snowdrift, too,
has lost its beauty to shadows.
Not removing the camera from my pocket,
I plan to return to the boat ramp
the next day
at the same time.

Yet I know
the beauty of the sunlight
playing musically on the snowdrifts
has disappeared
forever.

In my mind I retain a vivid picture
of the Door County snowdrifts.
I often pull it out
and sink into its awesome creation.

Indian Village

The last Indian village in the city
nestled on a quiet wooded bluff where
today 26th Street crosses the expressway.

You could see campfires flickering there
and along the adjacent river valley
until 1838, a few years
after the Army had marched most of the
tribes west for good, along the Trail of Tears.

Known as "Lime Kiln Ridge,"
you still see limestone there.
But now the red leaves are off the sumac:
There's a pall in autumn's gun-metal gray air
and cars roar by blind to the fires that
in summer sparked and
glowed orange against the sky;
whose embers rose on the gentle air to fly.

A Tree and Its Seasons

Amidst the darkest phases
           of the evening shadows
Stands an unbending tree,
Living inside its age,
Existing around its wisdom.

With spring, upon the arrival
           of warmth and rain,
The tree unveils a young, green, fresh
Covering of leaves
In silent humbleness.

And after a life-giving,
           abundant summer's growth
Its leaves, in final farewell,
Blossom into brilliant color,
Fade, then fall in silence
           to the ground.

Against the crystal blue,
           autumn sky with clouds,
The stark branches of the tree
Remain determined in their upward reach
And beautiful in their blue-black contrast.

Although all leaves are gone
           and lay damp and brown,
While the wind rushes through
The limbs, I, gazing upward,
Feel no sadness, only strength.

The Chickadees' Revenge

Every day the red squirrel dominates
the sunflower seeds.
Bigger than five chickadees,

he audaciously sits down on top of the seed pile,
and eats his fill.
When finished

he wanders off satisfied—fatter than yesterday! But
today it's the
chickadees' revenge.

I put the seeds out for all. But the chickadees
are awake early,
swooping like fighter pilots.

Sunflower seeds their targets, the battle for food
commences
roaring on and on

until the enemy hunger is vanquished; the birds fly
swiftly home.
All is quiet for a short time.

Then at 9:30 a.m., the red squirrel, up late from his
hibernation, deftly jumps
onto the porch, sniffing around.

"Here I am. Hey, where are my seeds?"
he seems to say.
Only shells remain.

Thinking someone has slipped up, he scampers
from the corner
to the pile of shells

and looks around as if to say,
"Is this a joke?"
He jumps onto a cedar,

hangs on its side, head stuck out parallel
to the porch,
waiting.

"No seeds forthcoming?" he seems to ask.
Running down the trunk,
back to the corner, in dis-

belief, he bolts for the snow-covered brush and
home. But no chickadees
anywhere to claim

their deserved revenge.

Experience Born

I saw you thinking,
Like a small bare tree.
I was part of the
Older one above.

It was a thought of
A life grown good,
A late left fear and
A new found love.

Then I saw you
As you walked away
From the wisdom spot,
Slowly but steadily.

And you looked up to me
In a smile sweet
Showing that you knew
With eyes that did see.

My great arms and hand
Like a sturdy branch,
Swept down to embrace
This newborn child.

I know that I smiled,
Though now I weep,
For you met my touch
Sudden and wild.

Man at the Nursing Home

By the window in a wheelchair was a man.
He asked, "Is that Marquette University?
Get as much education as you can,"

he said then. I pulled the drape and saw his hand.
"I got passage from Ireland for free,"
from his wheelchair by the window said the man,

"and worked awhile in Quebec as a farmhand.
After that I came here to Milwaukee." Get as much
education as you can—

the words had an enlightening ring to them
as they were said, almost recited, to me
near the window from a wheelchair by a man.

"I got a job at a downtown hotel, then
worked twenty-five years in a foundry—
you get as much education as you can."

I looked at his grey hair and his hand again.
Those words sunk deep into my memory
by the window near his wheelchair. Said the man,
"Get as much education as you can."

My Rushing Water

Dark green leaves cover the auburn water of
the river as it winds, cascading
across the plain. Muddy banks host old
trees; dusty autumn air hangs over
the water clear. The late day sunlight
highlights the trees' reds and golds and oranges. And
I gaze upon my rushing water thinking:
how long ago I played by that river.
The forest was my companion; I knew
every tree, every glen, every green knoll by
the river's edge, every stepping stone, every
branch leaning over the caramel-colored
water, the brush in the meadow, the sumac
on the other shore. I cannot go there
anymore for the past flows painfully through
my veins. The house on the hillside with its pillared
pane glass; the Lannon stone chimney, the tin
gray porch and the young birches that dance
dry leaves across the driveway in autumn—
these I can live no more, though I love them still.

Nuthatch Versus the Chickadees: The Battle for the Sunflower Seeds

Having had the bird feeder to themselves,
the chickadees flew in to find,

a red-breasted nuthatch, stripe on his eye,
stalwart on the summit of the feeder.

Making a stand for the store of sunflower seeds,
the nuthatch means trouble for th' chickadees.

Not seeing him at first—or are they simply
    slighting him?—
the chicks make a run for their cache.

But the long-beaked, dapper-blue intruder awaits them;
they suddenly veer at the sight.

As if hitting an invisible brick wall of resistance,
chickadees are repulsed left and right.

Retreating to a cedar tree *en group*
the chickadees seem to plan an attack:

"Two go together," their leader explains.
"The first one dives to divert him;

the second goes for the seed.
Alternate and continue on!"

he instructs masterfully.
And the battle plan succeeds!

But soon, without reason, the chickadees
grow weary of working together.

Reverting to single attacks,
the nuthatch handily fends them off.

A fast flyer and strong,
bigger than a chickadee,

the aggressor nuthatch becomes King of the Feeder!
and winner of the Sunflower Seed War.

The Pigeon River

I thought I'd take a walk alone,
an early December morning.
The air drew damp into my lungs;
the trees stood gray; the leaves crushed and brown;
the limestone blue and cold.

I took the West River Trail,
striding near the brown water's banks,
and halting atop a sparsely wooded ridge
listening for the elk or the woodpecker or the owl
but all was still.

*****

I thought someone had cut
into the tree trunks with a hatchet,
then realized a beaver had been at work.
Looking over the swift water,
I saw his dam.

In the middle of the river
partitioning the flow in its makeshift way;
it looked haphazard,
the logs strewn around on the watery island,
as if it didn't matter.

On the ridge the beaver's tree-felling work lay half done—
his teeth had torn away chunks near the bases
of a small forest of trees.
Looking like a collection of hour glasses,
some had yet to fall.

68

I waited silently,
hoping to behold the beaver at his work.
But nothing moved save the water
sweeping around the sand-banked bend
and the wind of December.

Two Birds

A bird on the porch this morning, a wren,
flew down the cornice, jumped the rail then
danced on the planks until joined by its mate.
Quickly both birds puffed themselves up a bit
and, with a strut, mounted the air and were gone.
Flying next door to the neighbor's blue-green lawn,
they joined a dozen others already there
who, bracing themselves against the autumn air,
resembled twelve small brown-gray balls of down
half blown, half flying, staying close to the ground.
I'm grateful to see these sweet birds now and then.
They remind me of Nature's blessings again.
Nature ever reminds me of Him who gives
His love, His life, and His light to all that lives.

Lake Michigan Shore

The snow settles on
the brittle fallen leaves,
the leaves on the cold green grass.

The sun cool in the
pink azure white gray rose sky.
Winter wind blowing across

the lake with white caps,
gulls, and slate-colored waves.
Mergansers snorkeling for fish.

Sometimes spray on the
window, the house near the
shore with the cedars and brush,

white pine, hemlock, yew,
birch, thimble berry, beech
completely barren, once lush.

No protection from
the wind at all this
time of year: not winter, not fall,

but cold and fresh. The
air from north or west
whipped by the wind. Snow squall

battering house with
flakes, damp and big, to tell
new season's approach to all.

Like summer but white
quiet, like spring but cool,
like autumn with sea gulls

screeching for fish and
spying on them. But how
do they see them from so

high? Flying, circling,
diving hard, hit water
at high speed. The fish below,

probably schooling.
Unannounced, the gull
breaks water on surface. Lo!

The cold fish is gone.
Can the others feel "gone"?
Without thinking we can know.

Running Through Air

When I was a child
I ran fast and wildly.
I thought, "I can keep running
Faster and faster—faster and
Faster still and faster...."

My feet whirled;
Up   up   up   up,
  down   down   down

My small shoes flew,
Tapping on the pavement.

I dived into the air;
I cut space.

It was nothing, really, anyhow,
That light, clear,
Untouchable tiny, tiny air.

I'd try to look at that clarity, too!
Nothing was so clear
Not a glass nor minor
Could be so clean, so light,
So pure, so fine—like music.

Simple to Sublime

She asked, "Do you like the rain or the snow?"
Her question surprised me and I said, "Well, yes,"
attempting a joke. But I really didn't know.
"I'd have to say I like them both." I guess

I surprised her then, along with myself.
I realize now I like all kinds of weather
because the body is only a shell
in which the mind and soul reside together,

and that the soul occupies the body
this incarnation, to work out certain desires
and has occupied many bodies previously:
male, female; black, white. After one expires,

the soul, for a karmically-determined time,
resides in the astral world of light and energy
and then incarnates again and finally
finds its way back Home to Eternal Joy.

In the Woods Near Water

She walked with me over
To a darkening wood.
Silent summer sky flowed fully
Above the trees that stood
Where the girl grasped my soul
And tore trembling at my heart.
A dangerous wind blew,
Warning the animals
To be on the alert.
Woman looked up to me.
While she smiled, her eye drank the moon
That gleamed at my shoulder.

Later, she hummed softly
A made-up little tune.

Washing the Car

There's something about
washing the car.

I gather the materials and tools together—
pail, soap, mitt,
sponge, rag, cloth,
chamois, vacuum,
glass and vinyl cleaner.

I spray the car all over
with fresh clear water.

Dipping the mitt into the pail,
then onto the car,
white suds swish over the surface
floating away the grit and grime.

I wash the front, hood, sides;
roof, rear, tires;
mirrors and glass.

Get ready for the inside!
I wash the windshield,
and the windows,

wipe the vinyl and the dash,
clean the seats and rugs.

Now she's done!
I pour out the water,

regroup my tools,
and put them away.

When I open the door,
to step inside,
the car feels like new.

I roll down the window.

Turning the key in the ignition,
I start the engine;
it rumbles softly under the hood.

I slide the gearshift into reverse,
crane my neck to look behind,
and slowly back down the driveway
into the road.

Water drips off from underneath.

I change the gearshift to drive.
My foot resting on the pedal,
I gradually accelerate.

A warm breeze is blowing
against my face;
sunlight fills the car.

As I drive, tires heavy atop the asphalt,
I am singing to Saturday.

Cinquains

Number 1

It hurt
when the boy put
his heavy boot down hard
and crushed the little bumble bee
so sweet.

Number 2

The light
from the orange sun
suddenly pierced the sky
over the roof—a gray slab of
concrete.

Number 3

I saw
a black cricket
fall over on its side
then get up again and hop at
the wall.

Salute to the Northern Clime

O northern clime I salute you
for your change of seasons, always four.
Winter summoned by autumn's leafy hand
that grows no longer for a winter's rest
after glowing from green to gold and then
from reds to browns and finally falling
to be shuffled by children as they walk.
O autumn nights so clear, so crisp
that leave the frosty pumpkin cold
staying until the morning light
comes to illuminate the reddish hills;
the deep-blue water by the shore;
the gold fields that the harvest left;
the blackened trees; the birches white;
the geese on their powerful wingéd flight.

O northern clime I salute you
with your white pure coat in winter that
makes everything infinite the same—
the snow that blankets the barren fields
and covers like a carpet the half-hidden hills:
the air so frosty, so chillingly cold;
the water so black and rushing along
or frozen blue and still for a while;
the nights so calm and eternally silent
with nothing to be seen but the cold white stars.
The dusk so soon, the day so short;
the morning storm that doubles the snow;
the whitish skies that cover the sun
seemingly forever 'til the storm passes through
and the cities and countrysides awaken anew.

O northern clime I salute you—
your summery days that last so long;
your hot small sun, your cathedral light
that shines ray-like through the leafy shade;
the blossoming flowers of orange, or red
that burst out blooming every day;
the birds a-wing that chirp and sing and
mimic the children's care-free play which
in turn fills the neighborhood 'til dusk;
the soft gray moon that swiftly rises
to throw its light across the high night clouds;
the warm night air humid with scent
of trees and grass and flowers and fields;
in the early morning silent stillness,
the birds that are quieted by your
dew-wrought coolness.

O northern clime I salute you—
with spring that seems so far away
yet suddenly blooms with a balmy air;
that ignites the sleeping giant buds while
the flowers awake from a dormant slumber;
the birds fly back from their southern homes
to flutter and dance on the spongy grass;
the bees wake up to a new spring world—
their buzzing at first seems so strange in the air;
the little brooks so clean with snow;
the tiny green plants that peak through the soil
to see if at last it's all right to come out.
The lake unfrozen; the north wind gone;
the loving rain and the tanager's song.

About the Author

Richard A. Bowen is author of ten books on self-help, autobiographical, history, and poetry. He works in business and industry as a topical writer and blogger, and currently lives in Wisconsin with his wife, author Karen A. Bowen, and their pets. Learn more at www.RichardABowen.com